Contents

1. **What is business letter writing?**   1
   Why do I need business letter writing skills?   2
   What are the key things to consider when writing business letters?   3
   Why would I write a business letter?   4
   What are the alternatives to writing a letter?   4
   What preparation do I need to do?   5

2. **How do I structure my business letter?**   6
   How long should a business letter be?   6
   What are the elements of a business letter?   6
   How do I lay out a letter?   8
   How do I structure a letter?   10
   How do I use headings?   10
   How do I address the recipient?   11
   How do I sign a letter?   14
   How do I refer to enclosures, additional pages and copies?   15

3. **What about language, grammar and punctuation?**   17
   What are the elements of good grammar?   17
   How do I deal with jargon and abbreviations?   20
   How do I use punctuation?   21
   How do I use numbers, acronyms and abbreviations?   23
   How do I keep sentences short and to the point?   25
   How do I get the reader interested?   27
   What tone and style should I use?   29
   What tense should I use?   30
   What language should I avoid?   31
   How do I use the features on a word-processor?   33
   How do I check a letter before sending it?   34

3. What other types of business letter should I know about?   **35**

What is a sales letter?   35

How do I respond to a letter of complaint?   37

What about an unjustified letter of complaint?   38

How do I write a letter of complaint?   40

Are there any rules for letters to non-English speakers?   41

4. Where can I find out more?   **42**

What publications could I look at?   42

Is there any special training?   43

Who could I contact?   43

Business Letter Writing

your questions and answers

Josy Roberts

TROTMAN

About the Author

Josy Roberts has worked in administrative, marketing and management roles over the last 15 years for a variety of organisations, including family-owned small businesses, charities and major corporations. As well as the scars of experience she holds an honours degree in Sociology, a marketing certificate and Diploma in Management.

She believes strongly that the success of organisations and individuals – whatever they do – is based on communications skills and a professional approach, and with that the working day can and should be enjoyable.

This first edition published in 1998 in Great Britain by Trotman and Company Limited, 12 Hill Rise, Richmond, Surrey TW10 6UA
© Trotman and Company Limited 1998

British Library Cataloguing in Publication Data
A catalogue record for this book is available from the British Library
ISBN 0 85660 326 0

Printed and bound in Great Britain by Redwood Books

1. What is business letter writing?

A business letter is a formal communication between people or organisations who are involved in trading – exchanging money for goods or services.

Writing a business letter is about developing that trade, so it is important to remember that a business letter is an official document. Of course there are many other communications between people and companies, for instance telephone conversations, email, meetings, presentations, contracts, orders and invoices. A business letter is the most powerful communications tool for providing structured and considered information in a formal way.

Among the many definitions, a 'letter' according to the Oxford English Dictionary is 'a missive, communication in writing addressed to a person or body of persons, an epistle. Also in extended use applied to certain formal documents issued by persons in authority'. Business letters are serious – unlike your Christmas thank you letters or postcards written on holiday. The chairman of ICI wouldn't write to his mother on company stationery and say he'd had a nice week at work.

In 1997 the Post Office estimated that of the 72 million items of post they delivered daily 80% were business communications. Business letters are business tools – they are used to provide or request information, confirm less formal communications or highlight a problem that needs to be resolved. The business letter presented on company stationery is an official communication, and can be legally binding in disputes between companies and individuals.

Business letters are used for important communications – the most serious example might be the declaration of war Chamberlain sent to Adolph Hitler in 1939. Of course very few people are given the task of writing declarations of war.

Business letter writing is not a new invention. Here is an example of a colourful missive – a translation of the Amarna letters – written in the 14th century BC to the Pharaoh of Egypt.

> Say to the King my Lord: Message of Zitriyara, your servant. I fall at the feet of the King, my Lord, seven times and seven times, both on the back and on the stomach.
>
> As I am a servant of the King, my Lord, he has obeyed the orders that the King, my Lord sent to his servant. I am the servant of the King my Lord.
>
> As the King is like the sun from the sky Samuma, we are unable to ignore the order of the King, my Lord, and we obey the commissioner that you have placed over me.

In this letter, Zitriyara accepts a new boss and way of doing business. In 35 centuries, grammar, typography and social convention have changed, and meetings and letters don't generally start with protestations and prostrations of obedience. But Zitriyara wrote the letter in a style that was appropriate for the reader, and he conveyed an important message.

Why do I need business letter writing skills?

A business letter is an important document.

❑ It deals with a trade issue.
❑ It shows the professionalism of both the writer and the company.
❑ It is likely to be saved and filed by the sender and the receiver so it must be an accurate record.

So writing a business letter well helps you and your company to be successful. Often a business letter is the first formal document a business contact receives – and the impression it gives creates opinions about the company and the writer. Think about how you feel when you read a restaurant menu that has not been translated well and has a lot of mistakes. Writing a business letter badly is worse than not sending one at all. Look at the next example.

Mr Rihcard Branston
Vergin Express
Heathrow airport

Dr Mr Pickle

I would lke to become an air pilot and wondered if you have jobs going in your company. I like planes allot and a man at British Airways told me to contact you.

What are the key things to consider when writing business letters?

'Those who write clearly have readers, those who write obscurely have commentators.' Albert Camus, *Notebooks* 1942–51

To write a good business letter you must:

❑ Use appropriate layout – with all the formal elements, the right titles and addresses.
❑ Ensure the content of your letter is correct and relevant.
❑ Use clear English – the correct grammar, and the right vocabulary.
❑ Make the style and tone of your writing appropriate for the reader, and the message you are sending.

The ability to write business letters well is necessary for career development into management or specialist positions. Could you imagine a government minister or a company director being successful if he or she couldn't write letters?

Why would I write a business letter?

There are many reasons to write a business letter – to seek information or opinion, to place or confirm an order, to sell a company's products, to offer information in response to an enquiry, to provide a quotation for a product or service, to make a complaint or to respond to complaint. Generally though, you have a business problem to solve.

Here are some examples:

❑ An individual has telephoned your company and asked for a brochure or details of your products and services.

❑ A customer has written a letter complaining about a product or service provided by your company.

❑ You are responding to a job advertisement in a newspaper.

❑ A meeting has been arranged by telephone and the details of the time, where it will take place, and the people attending need to be confirmed.

❑ You have been to a meeting and the client asked for more information on a subject.

❑ A supplier has provided a helpful service, and your company wants to offer formal thanks.

What are the alternatives to writing a letter?

A business letter takes time and money to produce – it needs to be written, printed, copied, posted, and filed. If you count up the time and resources used that could cost a company between £10 and £25 for each letter!

If simple questions need answering it is often faster and more effective to telephone or send an email. Think about the person you are communicating with. What is the most convenient way for them to receive information? A telephone call confirming a price or a date is much simpler and quicker – but do they need that confirmation in writing before they can act on the information? Do you need to keep a copy of a letter on file as a record of what you have said or done?

At the other end of the scale, if there is a great deal of material to send a report or face-to-face presentation would be better. For example, if you work for an events management company and you want to tell a potential client who is organising a staff hospitality day about the range of services you offer, a face-to-face presentation that allows discussion of their needs will be much more effective than a letter.

What preparation do I need to do?

Before you start to write a letter, plan what message needs to be conveyed and research all the back-up information you need.

WHO – Who are you writing to – is he or she the right person to deal with your query? Do you know the correct spelling of their name and address? Are you the right person to write the letter? Should someone else sign it?

WHAT – What are you writing about and why are you writing? Do you have all the facts you need – collect all the information you will be sending before you start writing. If your boss or colleague has asked you to write get a full briefing. If previous correspondence exists make sure you have it handy.

HOW – Plan the structure of the letter – write some notes on the key points to cover then read them through. Are they logical? Do they link in a sensible way? Is there anything missing or unnecessary?

DETAILS – Check whether your company has a style template for layout and get examples of other letters to copy.

2. How do I structure my business letter?

How long should a business letter be?

A business letter should be a maximum of one to two pages. Business letters are generally three or four paragraphs.

Remember that most people don't have the time to read lengthy prose – they have telephone calls, meetings and other demands on their day. The simpler and clearer the letter, the better results it will have.

If a lot of information is necessary it should be included as a report or brochure, unless it is a contract. For example, an architect or builder could write a proposal for constructing a house which would include detailed descriptions of the work to be carried out and costs, and the letter might be several pages long.

What are the elements of a business letter?

The diagram on the next page shows the structure of a business letter and the different elements it contains. These elements are generally organised in the order shown, but you will find many variations in letters you see at work. For instance, your company's house-style may be to put the date and reference before the address, or to put the title before the salutation.

Noah Shipbuilders Ltd
West Quay Road, Poole, Dorset
BH14 OTT
Telephone: 01202 673451
Registered No: 14133242

Mr Justin Thyme
Fleet Manager
Millennium Charters Ltd
Harbour View
PLYMOUTH   PL3 4XW

Ref: MIL/LID

1st July 1998

Dear Mr Thyme

Delivery of Lifeboat Order

The lifeboats ordered on 1st June 1998 by
Millennium Charters will be available for delivery
by 29th November 1999.

This is subject to our standard terms and
conditions that are set out in the booklet
enclosed.

Please confirm the delivery address and
the payment schedule you wish to follow.

Yours sincerely

Mary Nuwer
Sales Manager

Enc

Copies to: Peter Owte, Director

Heading or letter head.
Company address, contact
details, logo, and registered
number

Name and title. The person
you are writing to and their
business title
Address. Full postal address

Reference. The document
name for easy retrieval
Date. Date of writing

Salutation. Dear…

Title or heading. The subject
of the letter
First paragraph. Why you are
writing – the introduction
provides context for the reader

Body of the letter. Information
or message – each paragraph
should have a single message

Final paragraph. Action – ask
recipient to do something

Complimentary close

Signature and title. A space
for signature with your name
and business title beneath

Note of enclosures. Enc
shows further information is
included
Copies (or cc). If the letter is
copied to others list their names
and job titles.

How do I lay out a letter?

There are three 'standard' styles

❑ Blocked
❑ Semi-blocked
❑ Indented

The indented style is the traditional layout, but it can look old-fashioned now. Most companies use a fully blocked or semi-blocked style.

Fully blocked and semi-blocked styles use open punctuation. This means that commas are not used after each line of the address, the salutation, or the complimentary close. The indented style generally uses full punctuation in these places.

Many companies have a house-style – a standard way of laying out letters and other documents, and even a preferred typeface. This is chosen to compliment the letterhead and show corporate identity. When laying out a letter it is important to check whether a house-style exists for your company. If your company doesn't have any guidelines, then choose a standard layout for your own letters and be consistent.

BLOCKED

Name
Address
Postcode

Date

Salutation

Heading

Paragraph 1 Paragraph 1 Paragraph 1 Paragraph 1 Paragraph 1 Paragraph 1 Paragraph 1 Paragraph 1 Paragraph 1

Paragraph 2 Paragraph 2 Paragraph 2 Paragraph 2

Complimentary close

Signature
Title

In the most commonly used blocked style all elements of the letter are aligned in the left-hand margin. This can appear lopsided – particularly if the letter is short.

SEMI-BLOCKED

Name   Date
Address
Postcode

Salutation
                          Heading
Paragraph 1 Paragraph 1 Paragraph 1 Paragraph 1 Paragraph
1 Paragraph 1 Paragraph 1 Paragraph 1 Paragraph 1

Paragraph 2 Paragraph 2 Paragraph 2 Paragraph 2 Paragraph
2 Paragraph 2 Paragraph 2

Complimentary close

> The semi-blocked style aligns
> the date to the right-hand margin
> and centres the heading (and
> sometimes the complimentary
> close and signature) to give a
> more balanced appearance.

Signature
Title

INDENTED

Name,   Date
Address,
Postcode

Salutation,
                          Heading
    Paragraph 1 Paragraph 1 Paragraph 1 Paragraph 1
Paragraph 1 Paragraph 1 Paragraph 1 Paragraph 1
Paragraph 1

    Paragraph 2 Paragraph 2 Paragraph 2 Paragraph 2
Paragraph 2 Paragraph 2 Paragraph 2

                Complimentary close,

                Signature
                Title

> The indented style is more
> traditional but rarely used now.
> The first line of every paragraph is
> indented four spaces. Headings
> are centred and closures are
> aligned left on a central point.

How do I structure a letter?

If you are writing a letter to request information or send information the pneumonic STRIPE is an easy structure to follow:

S Salutation

T Topic (your heading)

R Reason – why are you writing

I Information – request or include specific data

P Prompt to Action – ask the reader to do something or confirm an action you will take

E End – add a complimentary close and your signature

See page 7 for a diagram of a standard layout that uses these elements.

How do I use headings?

It is always a good idea to provide a heading for your letter so the reader knows immediately what it is about. Headings can refer to a specific document, or introduce the subject of the letter, for example:

<u>**Invoice Number 5673**</u>

or <u>**New Price List for Sandwich Service**</u>

Supplemental headings (subheadings) should be used with great care, and are only valuable in longer letters. They are similar to the titles of chapters in a book. If you are genuinely covering a new subject, signal it with a subheading and make sure that the overall heading of the letter covers the subheadings used.

How do I address the recipient?

There are three places in a letter to address the recipient – on the envelope, in the address at the top of the letter and in the salutation.

Address

In the address at the top of the letter and on the envelope use the reader's title, full name, business title and business address.

If you are responding to a letter from someone, copy how they refer to themselves and the address on their letterhead.

✔ Correct	✘ Incorrect
Mrs Diana Mond	Di Mond
Marketing Manager	Tiffanies
Tiffany & Co	25 Bond St
25 Old Bond St	W1
LONDON W1 2RW	

Salutation

The salutation depends on the relationship you have with the reader. If you have met the recipient or spoken to them on the phone it may be appropriate to address the letter with their first name:

Dear Diana or Dear Jim   ✔

If you haven't met or spoken with the recipient use the title and surname.

Dear Mrs Mond or Dear Mr Stone   ✔

If your recipient is female and you are not sure of her preferred title, it is acceptable to use 'Ms'. However, always use the correct title if you know it – whether Ms, Miss, Mr, Mrs, Dr, Professor or any of the special titles listed on the next page.

It is wrong to include both the reader's title, first name and surname in the salutation

Dear Mrs Diana Mond   ✘

But if you are not sure of the gender of the person you are writing to (and you can't find out easily), to avoid causing offence an alternative is to use first and last names without a title:

    Dear Chris Taile   ✔

A good rule of thumb is to be more rather than less formal when writing business letters. Some people, particularly more senior staff or older customers or clients, can be annoyed if a letter is overly familiar.

Decorations, Honours and Qualifications

Decorations, honours, qualifications and government titles follow the name in the address of a letter. Here are some examples.

Mrs A Star OBE	(Order of the British Empire)
Ms U Ramsbottom BA	(Bachelor of Arts)
Mr A Scargill MP	(Member of Parliament)
Mr R Estead JP	(Justice of the Peace)

Academic and professional qualifications are only used in formal correspondence but decorations and honours should always be used in addressing the letter.

Use of special titles

For most people the standard titles Mr, Mrs, Ms or Miss should be used in the address and salutation. However there are some important exceptions – professional and honorary titles.

Professional titles

Doctor	usually abbreviated to Dr	Dr V Small
Professor	sometimes abbreviated	Prof C Moore
		Professor C Moore
Military ranks	usually abbreviated	Lieut N Pillage
		Maj R Game
		Sqn-Ldr R Borne
The Reverend or Reverend	usually abbreviated	The Rev O Luton
		Rev N Geen

Knights and Peers

Titles of peers and knights have varying forms of address and salutations according to conventions. (You should omit the word 'Dear' before 'My Lord' in the salutation.)

Status	Address	Salutation
Baron	The Rt Hon Lord —	My Lord —
Baroness	The Rt Hon Lady —	Madam
Baronet	Sir Alfred Moxton BT	Sir
Bishop	The Right Rev the Lord Bishop of —	My Lord Bishop
Dame	Dame Edna Everage DBE	Madam
Duke	His Grace the Duke of —	My Lord Duke
Duchess	Her Grace the Duchess of —	Madam
Earl	The Right Hon the Earl of —	My Lord —
Countess	The Right Hon the Countess of —	Madam
Judge (County Court)	His Honour Judge —	Sir
Judge (High Court)	The Honourable Mr Justice —	Sir
Knight	Sir Felix Gato Kt	Sir
Prime Minister	The Right Hon Tony Blair PC MP	Sir
(or a female Prime Minister)	The Right Hon Margaret Thatcher PC MP	Madam
The Queen	Her Most Gracious Majesty, Queen Elizabeth II	Madam
Viscount	The Rt Hon the Viscount —	My Lord —
Viscountess	The Rt Hon the Viscountess —	Madam

Professional titles precede other titles, for example:

Admiral The Right Hon Lord

How do I sign a letter?

There are conventions that link the salutation of a letter with the complimentary close that must be followed.

If you are writing to a company and don't have a specific contact name for the salutation, use the complimentary close 'Yours faithfully'.

> Dear Sir   Dear Sirs
>
> Dear Madam   Dear Sir/Madam
>
>   Yours faithfully

If you are writing to a specific person, use the salutation 'Yours sincerely'.

> Dear Mr Call   Dear Ms Stake
>
> Dear Mrs Goodsmile   Dear Reverend Balderdash
>
>   Yours sincerely

Some people finish their letters using 'Yours truly' or 'Best wishes'. This is not accepted as formal business practice at the moment, but if you want to strike a more personal note, you could use a similar phrase before 'Yours sincerely'.

> With best wishes
>
> Yours sincerely

Beneath the complimentary close, six lines should be left for signature, then the writer's name should be typed, with their business title beneath.

> Yours sincerely
>
>
> Owen Paye
> Financial Director

Don't forget to sign the letter before you post it, as it is the signature that gives it authority. If you are signing a letter for someone else, the practice is to 'pp' it. Put your own signature above the writer's typed name, and write 'pp' next to the name. This is an abbreviation for the Latin term *per procurationem* – meaning by proxy, or on behalf of.

How do I refer to enclosures, additional pages and copies?

Enclosing information

It is likely you will be sending other material with a letter – for instance, a copy invoice, a brochure or price list. At the bottom of a letter type the abbreviation 'Enc' or 'Encs' if there are other items being sent.

Don't forget to put your enclosures in the envelope before posting – it's a mistake that too frequently happens. Even if you're in a hurry to catch the post, or have a lot to send out, make time to check each letter as you put it in the envelope and ensure any enclosures mentioned have been included.

Continuation sheets

If a letter goes beyond one page, the subsequent pages are called continuation sheets. They should not be printed on letterhead, but there are some conventions to obey.

It is good practice to indicate that a continuation sheet is provided with the following in the bottom right-hand corner:

.../continued

The top of the continuation page should show the recipient's name, the page number and date. For example:

Grey, Squirrel, Acorn & Co   -2-   21st October 1998

You should never use a continuation sheet just to include the complimentary close and signature. If less than two lines of text are going to appear on the second page then edit your letter to make it fit one page or add more space to put at least one paragraph on the continuation page.

Sending copies

Sometimes a copy of a letter is sent to a third party – perhaps a business partner or professional adviser who needs to be aware of any actions your have taken, or needs a copy of the correspondence for their records.

The receiver should be told who else is receiving a copy of the letter. You should indicate this by writing the names and companies at the foot of the letter, after the signature and 'Enc'. Use a 'Copies to:' or 'cc:' heading (cc stands for carbon copy – as this method of making copies is rare now, 'Copies to' is more often used).

Copies to:
Mr Duncan Vicar, Mead and Sons Ltd
Ms Estelle Tale, *News of the World*

3. What about language, grammar and punctuation?

What are the elements of good grammar?

Written English is more formal than the way we speak, so it is important to understand the rules of grammar when writing business letters. Most of the time you know instinctively what is right and wrong. Compare the following sentences:

Carol done real good at interview. Smith was blown away.

Carol impressed Mr Smith in the interview.

It is easy to tell which one is correct – and which one will create the best impression.

Here is an extract from a letter in the novel *Nicholas Nickleby*, by Charles Dickens:

> Sir,
> My pa requests me to write to you, the doctors considering it doubtful whether he will ever recuvver the use of his legs which prevents his holding a pen...

Badly written letters are a great source of humour – but they leave a poor impression, and they won't get your message across.

A review of word types

Words are the building blocks of writing. Grammar is about getting the right type of word in the right place in your sentences.

Noun	Names something – tree, book, sunshine, community
Proper noun	Names a specific place or person and is capitalised – Peter, Frankfurt, Boy Scouts
Pronouns	Are used instead of nouns – there are four types: *Personal* – I, we, you, they *Relative* – who, whose, that, which *Demonstrative* – that, this, those, these *Indefinite* – any, each, several, some
Adjectives	Describe nouns – *sunny* day, *enormous* dog
Verbs	The doing words which describe the action – *talks, talking, talked; eats, eating, ate*
Adverbs	Modify the verb – eating *slowly*, laughing *quietly*
Prepositions	Show connections – into, from
Conjunctions	Connect words or phrases in more complex sentences – and, but, yet, for, then, next

If you are unsure about the rules of good grammar, there are many useful books available. A selection is listed on page 42.

Sentence structure

The simplest sentence must have a subject that performs a main action on an object.

Subject	**Action**	**Object**
Carol	impressed	Mr Smith

Subjects and objects are generally nouns or pronouns – these are people, things or places. Action words are verbs, and they are the central pin of the sentence. There are three ways of describing verbs:

- ❑ tense
- ❑ first, second or third person
- ❑ singular or plural

A verb tense describes *when* the action happens:

Present	He studies
Past	He studied
Future	He will study
Conditional	He would study

First person	I, we
Second person	you
Third person	he, she, it, they

The main subject determines whether a verb is singular or plural:

He runs
They run

The ability to write well means taking the basic grammar a step forward and becoming competent at writing more complex sentences that link ideas, and avoiding repetition. The following example shows how short sentences can appear childish and repetitive.

'The Executive Committee governs the Trust. The Executive Committee has set up an inquiry. They think complaints may show administrative failings.'

Sentences should deal with one concept and make sense on their own. In the above example there is only one key point; the secondary facts are background information. To support the key point these can be included as clauses.

'The Executive Committee, governing body of the trust, has launched an inquiry into whether recent complaints show significant administrative failings.'

How do I deal with jargon and abbreviations?

The English language is extremely rich and varied. It is also live – which means new words are invented all the time, or new uses for existing words become generally accepted. In business and business writing this is particularly true: you have probably heard or read about 'buzzwords', jargon and TLAs (three letter acronyms).

Buzzwords are words and phrases that become fashionable because they represent new ideas or concepts, and get taken up and used by journalists and commentators. Here are recent examples of buzzwords:

Empowerment Giving employees authority and self-determination.

Downsizing Reducing the number of people or size of a company.

Coopetition Cooperating with a competitor for mutual benefit.

Edutainment Educational products that are fun.

Infotainment Information products that are fun.

Straw man An idea put forward so it can be attacked.

Globoboss A cosmopolitan executive who can perform well around the world.

Emoticon Symbol made up of punctuation marks that resembles a human expression, especially used in emails.

In practice every specialist area has its own vocabulary, or jargon. For example, marketing professionals talk and write about FMCGs (fast moving consumer goods), through-the-line campaigns, USPs (unique selling propositions), and the list goes on.

If you want to use special words decide whether the reader will understand them. If you are writing to someone in the same field then using words with specific technical meaning appears professional and helps keep your writing concise. Don't use words or jargon that you don't understand yourself – it will be immediately obvious to the reader.

Abbreviations help avoid repetition or very ponderous sentences. When using abbreviations or acronyms it is good practice to provide a definition the first time it is used. For example:

'Our company has ten years' experience of developing and managing Wide Area Networks (WANs) for a range of business clients. In the specification stage we will define the performance requirements of the WAN for your business.'

How do I use punctuation?

There are two ways to think about punctuation – firstly the overall style of letter where standard rules apply, and secondly as an essential part of good sentence structure to aid readability.

Open punctuation is now generally accepted practice – so punctuation marks are only used in the main body of the letter (see page 8).

Here is a quick checklist of punctuation symbols, and how they should be used.

■ Fullstop   Fullstops are used at the end of a complete
                  sentence, in some abbreviations and when numbers
                  are expressed in decimals.

■ Commas   Commas are used as pause marks to separate lists,
                  or sentence clauses.

                       The service includes monthly statements, a free
                       help-line, discounts on additional orders and 30
                       days' free credit.

                       To finish the proposal by the deadlines set, we will
                       need additional information.

; Semicolons — Semicolons provide longer pauses than commas and are used in compound sentences

> There is no reason to doubt the report's conclusions; the data has been checked.

: Colon — The colon is used to introduce the next phrase or item such as a dependent item, a quote or a list.

> The following ingredients will be necessary: flour, milk, eggs, butter and vanilla.

? Question mark — The question mark is an alternative to a full stop and should be used after a direct question.

> Will you be placing an order this month?

! Exclamation marks — Exclamation marks should be used at the end of a sentence to show strong emotion or humour. They are rarely appropriate in business letters.

' Quotation marks — Quotation marks are used before and after actual words spoken or quoted.

> Mr Davies has stated that 'the service provided was slow and inadequate'.

' Apostrophe — Apostrophes are used in two ways: to show possession, and in contractions

> Mrs Chippendale's table was returned.
> She didn't want to keep it.

(Contractions are usually avoided in business letters as they are considered too informal.)

(Parenthesis — Parentheses, also called brackets, are used to show explanatory material.

> It is clear that all learning must imply memory (that is storage of previously acquired information).

Parentheses can be used to frame numbers or letters in text.

(1) research; (2) preparation; (3) development...

They are also used to frame letters or numbers that have been written in full.

Confederation of British Industry (CBI)

One hundred thousand pounds (£100,000)

■ Dash   Dashes are used as separators to show a change of ideas – they are not an alternative to commas, semicolons or full stops.

■ Hyphen   Hyphens are used to divide a word at the end of the line or as part of a compound word (for example, 'tailor-made', 'north-east'). Try not to break words at the end of lines as this can look messy, but if you cannot avoid it, use a dictionary to check correct hyphen breaks.

■ Omission marks   Also called an ellipsis, these are used to show that words are missing if a direct quote is given.

How do I use numbers, acronyms and abbreviations?

Numbers and dates

Numbers are frequently included in business letters. There may be some rules in your company's house-style, but if not you should follow these as guidelines for common practice:

❑ Generally one to ten are written in full (two letters, five cups of coffee), 11 onwards can be provided in digits for easier reading (for example, 62,539,754 rather than sixty-two million, five hundred and thirty-nine thousand, seven hundred and fifty four!)

❑ Never start a sentence with a string of numbers.

❑ Use a comma to break the thousands and millions only when the figure is five digits or more, eg 2500 to 25,000.

❑ Fractions should be written in full – three-quarters, two-thirds etc.

❑ Percentages should be represented numerically – 10%, 23%.

❑ Round numbers should be written in full, eg one hundred, one million.

For dates, some companies have a style preference, so check the version in use, for example:

> Friday, 17th July 1998
>
> 17 July 1998
>
> July 17, 1998

Abbreviations

Standard abbreviations are listed in most dictionaries – here are some of the most commonly used in business letter writing.

Fullstops are sometimes used when a word or phrase has been abbreviated, but this is becoming less common. Your company may have a policy on this, so check first. Here are a few examples of typical abbreviations.

e.g. *or* eg	for example *(exempli gratia)*
etc. *or* etc	and so on *(et cetera)*
Enc. *or* Enc	enclosure
i.e. *or* ie	that is *(id est)*
p.s. *or* ps	postscript

Some words are abbreviated by initial or contracted (for example, Ltd is a contraction of Limited, and Mr of Mister) – and these can be written without fullstops.

c/f	carried forward
c/o	care of
Inc	Incorporated
Ltd	Limited
Dr	Doctor
p/l	profit and loss
pa	per annum
re	with reference to
ref	reference

rsvp	please answer (short for the French *répondez, s'il vous plaît*)
vat	value added tax
w/e	week ending

It is very common for companies and associations to use an acronym, which is a word made up from the initial letters of their name. These are generally written without fullstops. For example:

BA	British Airways
BBC	British Broadcasting Corporation
DTI	Department of Trade and Industry
IBM	International Business Machines

Before you include an acronym in a letter check that the organisation uses it to describe themselves. For example, is it in their logo? Is it in their brochure or letters?

How do I keep sentences short and to the point?

Review the phrases you have used for clichés and unnecessary words. Check that your sentence communicates a single idea. Use simple words when simple words will do, and if you need to check clarity use the fog factor calculation.

Fog Factor

The 'fog factor' is a quick measure of readability. It is based on research which shows that long words and long sentences make writing difficult to understand. As a general rule, a sentence over 25 words is too long.

You calculate the fog factor by:
❑ counting the number of words with three or more syllables
❑ counting the number of sentences
❑ dividing the number of words counted by the number of sentences.

Aim for a fog factor that doesn't exceed 4.

An <u>unusual</u> and <u>elegantly</u> <u>designed</u> two <u>bedroomed</u>, freehold <u>property</u>, set within this <u>delightfully</u> <u>exclusive</u> <u>development</u>, <u>ideally</u> placed for access to <u>transportation</u> and public <u>amenities</u>. 11

The <u>accommodation</u>, which has been <u>extensively</u> <u>remodernised</u> with <u>exquisite</u> flair, <u>comprises</u> two double bedrooms, <u>luxurious</u> en-suite bathroom <u>facilities</u>, spacious <u>reception</u> room and fully fitted <u>designer</u> kitchen. 9

Fog factor 11 + 9 ÷ 2 = 10

When letting a <u>property</u> for the first time there are often issues where <u>potential</u> landlords need advice. 2

Brown's offer a <u>professional</u> no-fee <u>advisory</u> service geared to <u>answering</u> simple and complex questions about <u>property</u> rental. 4

For more <u>information</u> on Brown's <u>management</u> service, <u>telephone</u> your local office listed below. 3

Fog factor 2 + 4 + 3 ÷ 3 = 3

So, the best way to reduce the fog factor is to use simple words when simple words will do. Here are some examples:

abundance	lot	forward	send
alteration	change	fundamental	basic
anticipate	expect	generate	produce
appreciable	a lot	initiate	start, begin
authentic	true	locality	place, area
beneficial	helpful	merchandise	goods
considerable	much	numerous	many
commencement	start, beginning	obtain	get
communicate	tell	optimum	best
cooperation	help	practically	nearly
correspond	write	proceed	go
deficiencies	shortages	problematical	doubtful
dispatch	send	requirements	needs, wants
discontinue	end	residence	home
duplicate	copy	state	say
emphasise	stress	sufficient	enough
encounter	meet	termination	end
endeavour	try	utilise	use
envisage	imagine	viable	practical, possible
finalise	finish, complete		

How do I get the reader interested?

Using headings and opening paragraphs

Most people only take a few minutes to skim a letter – so the heading or title and opening sentence of your letter is key.

Make sure the title explains simply but fully what your letter is about. In the first sentence tell the reader exactly why you are writing to them, so the reader immediately understands why it is relevant to him or her. Compare these examples:

Dear Mrs Jones		Dear Mrs Jones
<u>Lower telephone charges</u>		<u>Changes in published rates</u>
I am writing to tell you that Connect plc is amending its local call rates which will reduce your monthly bill.		Connect plc have reviewed the current rate card and decided to make adjustments.

Using language

Active and passive language

In the active voice, the subject of a sentence performs the action.

> 'My manager agrees to offer you an additional discount.'

But if the subject of the sentence that you are writing about is being acted upon, the passive voice may be more appropriate.

> 'The discount you requested has been agreed by my manager.'

The passive voice sounds more formal and objective and is often used (and overused) in business letters. The active voice is much livelier and easier to read. A passive verb says something has happened: it was agreed, it is decided, they were discussed, it has been given.

> 'I was sorry to hear that the adventure tour of The Old Kent Road was not enjoyable.'

An active verb is more personal and indicates that the subject is live: we agree, I regret, we hope.

> 'I am sorry you did not enjoy the adventure tour of The Old Kent Road.'

Try to use the active voice when you can. Rearrange the sentence so the subject is the person you are writing to or thing you are writing about.

> 'I was confused by your letter of 26th November.'
>
> *Subject:* I   *Verb:* confused
>
> 'Your letter of 26th of November is confusing.'
>
> *Subject:* your letter   *Verb:* confusing

You can see that the active voice is easier to understand and respond to.

Adjectives and adverbs

Adjectives and adverbs can be very powerful and add style to writing but you must be careful not to overuse them.

> 'Thank you for so promptly supplying the extensive and detailed proposal for an innovative and exciting range of chic executive office accessories.'

One adverb to modify the verb or one adjective to describe the noun gives focus to the message. Are you thanking for speed or detail?

> 'Thank you for promptly supplying your proposal for office accessories.'
> 'Thank you for supplying your detailed proposal for office accessories.'

Metaphors and analogies

A metaphor is an imaginative rather than a literal description.

> 'Your letter was a bolt from the blue…'

An analogy is drawing a similarity between things (using the word 'like'):

> 'Thank you for your terms of business document. Like Little Red Riding Hood, I am not sure if we are dealing with grandmother or the wolf.'

Metaphors and analogies add colour and style but are open to misinterpretation and can be seen as pretentious. What you think is clever or funny may go over someone else's head, or strike the wrong tone. Only use these devices in relatively informal communications or when you know the recipient well.

What tone and style should I use?

Business letters will have different types of message to get across – so depending on the reason for writing the structure and tone of your letters will vary.

1. *Positive letters* are the easiest to write because you agree to do something – send information, money, products and services.
2. *Neutral letters* take a non-committal tone – for example letters of reference or credit.
3. *Adverse letters* are providing bad news, or refusing a request. They must be written very carefully so that the business relationship is not damaged.
4. *Influencing letters* sell ideas or products, and ask the reader to take some form of action.

Start by asking yourself what kind of letter you are writing.

Positive and neutral letters should be structured in the following way:
1. The main idea
2. Details or explanations
3. Close

Messages in positive letters can be reinforced using emotional words:

'I am *very pleased* to send you this revised quotation...'

'We *look forward* to starting this *exciting* project next month...'

But don't go to extremes. Which example below seems the most businesslike?

'Thank you for the invitation to your launch party on 15th August on Brighton Pier. Unfortunately I will be away at a conference, so am unable to attend. I hope you have a successful event.'

or: 'I was thrilled to receive the invitation to your exciting launch bonanza. Can you imagine my devastation when I realised it clashes with the tedious annual company meeting in ghastly Swindon?'

The wording of neutral letters should be more impassive.

> 'In reply to your letter of 5th August, we have always found Ms Renting to be a reliable employee, and know of no reason why she would make an unsuitable tenant for your property.'

Adverse or influencing letters which send an unwelcome message need to provide explanations first, rather than starting with a negative statement.

1. Neutral statement
2. Facts and reasons
3. Unwelcome message
4. Other ideas which take the emphasis away from the previous paragraph.

Look at some examples on page 37–39 for dealing with letters of complaint. If you are writing an adverse letter the specific relationship in place will direct how much empathy you need to offer the reader – and therefore the level of explanation needed and the amount of sympathy or apology to express.

For details on how to write influencing letters, see the advice given on pages 35–36.

What tense should I use?

Depending on the relationship with the person you are writing to and the subject, you will need to consider which tense is appropriate. For example, a letter written in the third person is more formal:

Dear Sirs

Invoice 156/04/1

Please re-issue the enclosed invoice, calculating the discount at the agreed rate of 10%.

Yours faithfully

Accounts Department

A letter written in the first person is appropriate for a closer relationship:

Dear Fiona

Proposal for a new company brochure

Thank you for spending time with our designers yesterday – the meeting was very productive.

I am writing to confirm that the additional print cost of including a pocket on the folder will be £1200 for a print run of 5000.

Please let me know if you wish to change your original order.

Yours sincerely

Frank Leigh
Sales Executive

What language should I avoid?

It can be tempting to use jargon, figures of speech or unnecessary words to make a business letter seem more formal. Here are some examples of overly formal phrases and figures of speech to avoid:

Watch out for	**Use an alternative**
Beginnings	
With reference to your letter of/Further to…	About, concerning
The above mentioned…	This
We acknowledge receipt of/ We are in receipt of...	We have received
Latin tags	
As per, per, per pro, protem, ibid, viz	*delete or use an English equivalent*

Wordiness

Due to the fact that…	Because of
On the occasion of…	On, when
In the event that…	If
With regard to/In respect of…	About, concerning, regarding
In the sum of…	Of
In the neighbourhood of…	Near
In recognition of the fact that…	About
Answer in the affirmative	Confirm
Permit me to say…	*don't use*
May we take this opportunity of…	
It will be appreciated that…	

Vague statements of dates

As soon as possible	Soon – *or be precise, give a date!*
In the not too distant future	
At your earliest convenience	

Endings

I have pleasure in enclosing herewith…	Here is, I enclose
Waiting the favour of your reply…, Trusting we may be favoured by receipt of….	Look forward to hearing from you
Assuring you of our best attention at all times….	

You can see that many of the phrases above appear overly formal, and there are simpler and clearer alternatives.

It is equally inappropriate to use overly familiar jokey language or slang in a business letter.

> Dear Tim
>
> Thanks a bunch for the great scoff at lunch the other day mate. My manager was well impressed.
>
> We don't want you to get in a tiff about extra charges – so here is my scam to sort it.

How do I use the features on a word-processor?

Word-processors provide the user with hundreds of features for laying out letters and changing typography. Unless you want your letter to look like you spent more time playing with the design features than writing, leave most of these alone.

The best advice is 'less is more'. For a readable and professional looking letter, stick to one font (typeface), and one font size throughout. Use bold and underlining for headings only, or to emphasise very important points. Don't embolden whole paragraphs as you will lose the impact. Italic can be used for names of publications, such as books and newspapers (eg *The Good Pub Guide, The Sunday Times*).

Only include tables, bulleted lists, diagrams or footnotes if they genuinely help make the meaning clearer. These are devices for longer, more complicated documents like reports or chapters in books.

Advanced word-processors have some very useful features. You can set page templates, automatically number and date pages and check spelling and grammar. These tools save you time, ensure your presentation is consistent and help to prevent errors, so make use of them whenever you can.

How do I check a letter before sending it?

At the beginning of this book we listed the four elements of business letter writing:

❑ Layout
❑ Content
❑ Grammar
❑ Style

When you have finished writing your letter you must carefully check all of these

1. Look at your layout – does it follow an established style, have you got all the elements in the right place?
2. Read once for grammar, punctuation and spelling.
3. Read for tense – are you consistent?
4. Check the meaning – is the content clear, and is the data correct? Does each paragraph have a single message? Do you have the enclosures ready? Remember that it is frustrating for the reader and gives a poor impression if enclosures are missing.
5. Imagine you are the reader who has had an extremely bad journey to work, there are 20 other letters on your desk and you only have 30 seconds for each. What impression does your letter give?

It is a very good idea to ask a colleague to read the letter too as a final check.

Remember that it takes more time to write a succinct letter than to capture all your thoughts on paper.

> 'I have made this [letter] longer than usual, only because
> I have not had time to make it shorter.'
>
> Blaise Pascal, *Lettres Provinciales* 1657

4. What other types of business letter should I know about?

What is a sales letter?

The sales process that drives a potential customer to a purchase your products is often described by the pneumonic AIDA.

A	Awareness	Did you know about the product?
I	Interest	Is it relevant to you?
D	Desire	Do you want it?
A	Action	How do you purchase it?

Companies write sales letters to move potential customers down this path.

Often the reader hasn't asked to be written to and may not have heard of you or your company before, so a sales letter needs to cover all of the points – simply and clearly.

There are some golden rules to apply:

❑ Make the letter relevant to the person who is receiving it.
❑ Clearly express the benefits and features your product offers.
❑ Be courteous – don't talk down to the reader or be overly informal.
❑ Keep the letter as concise as possible.

Using STRIPE (see page 10):

S	Salutation	Get the name right
T	Title	Explain the benefits you offer
R	Reason	Why you are writing, why it is relevant
I	Information	What backs up the benefits you promise
P	Prompt to Action	What the reader should do
E	End	Who you are

MOPS
Management of Premises Service
89 Bucket Street, Gare-on-Tees TY5 13P
01987 234590

Dear Office Manager

Save money on cleaning services

As an office manager you are probably faced with increasing costs for daily cleaning and rubbish disposal, combined with complaints from your colleagues about disruption to their working day.

MOPS can help you. We provide a professional cleaning service to freshen your offices on a daily or weekly basis. Working at night between 10pm and 6am, our staff provide an unobtrusive and thorough service – supervised by an experienced quality control manager.

We will save you the cost and headache of recruiting and managing out-of-hours staff and purchasing and maintaining expensive cleaning equipment.

I have enclosed a brochure which outlines our charging structure and the range of services MOPS offers. If you would like to arrange a meeting to discuss your needs in more detail, and a free quotation for services, please call me on 0117 8745 667.

Yours faithfully

Hugh Vere
Sales Manager

How do I respond to a letter of complaint?

If you need to reply to a letter of complaint – deal with it immediately, don't let it grow cold in your in-tray. The faster your company responds the more receptive the complainant will be.

First, make sure you are the right person to deal with the letter – do you have authority? Can you solve the problem they complain about? Can you guarantee that any actions you promise will be taken? If not, find the person who can deal with it and make sure they respond.

If you can deal with it, personalise your reply – to the sender and their problem – and make it relevant. Write a full letter that covers all their points – a tersely worded sentence could appear to be a brush off.

Don't tell the individual they are wrong. Don't blame a specific person or department – remember that you are representing the whole organisation, so you should write the letter accordingly.

The structure you should follow for each paragraph is:

1. Acknowledgement of the problem and sympathy for the distress the writer feels – without necessarily admitting responsibility.
2. Explain what happened to cause the problem.
3. Tell the reader what action will be taken in response to the complaint.
4. Restate your sympathy or apology, and express desire to retain their goodwill.

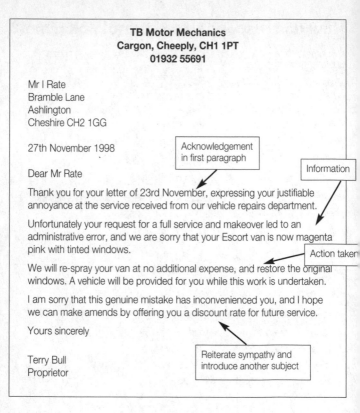

TB Motor Mechanics
Cargon, Cheeply, CH1 1PT
01932 55691

Mr I Rate
Bramble Lane
Ashlington
Cheshire CH2 1GG

27th November 1998

Dear Mr Rate

Thank you for your letter of 23rd November, expressing your justifiable annoyance at the service received from our vehicle repairs department.

Unfortunately your request for a full service and makeover led to an administrative error, and we are sorry that your Escort van is now magenta pink with tinted windows.

We will re-spray your van at no additional expense, and restore the original windows. A vehicle will be provided for you while this work is undertaken.

I am sorry that this genuine mistake has inconvenienced you, and I hope we can make amends by offering you a discount rate for future service.

Yours sincerely

Terry Bull
Proprietor

Callout labels: Acknowledgement in first paragraph · Information · Action taken · Reiterate sympathy and introduce another subject

What about an unjustified letter of complaint?

You may well need to write to an unsatisfied customer who is making a complaint where your company has genuinely not been at fault.

When you get a complaint, do some research. Find out how important the customer is to your company – do they spend £29.99 a year or several thousand pounds? Research the details behind the complaint – find out what has happened, and if they complain regularly.

If you have decided that their complaint is unjustified then prepare a letter that:

❑ acknowledges the problem
❑ provides information
❑ states your position (on behalf of your company)
❑ offers alternatives.

Witchford Lodge Hotel
Hauntley
Shropshire SH9 1FF

Mrs A Hough   5th June 1998
Office Manager
Machine Engineering Ltd
Holly Hampstead
Herts HR4 2XF

Dear Mrs Hough

I am responding to your letter of 2nd June, complaining about the residential training course you recently attended at our hotel. I am sorry you do not think the experience was value for money.

Your booking was made through the course organisers, Teachum, who are responsible for the content of the course and arrangements during the day.

Our records show that we did not experience a power cut for two days. The trainer on the course you attended instructed our staff to turn off all electrical appliances in the room for one hour, to avoid negative energy.

Teachum sets the inclusive price for the course, based on a group rate they negotiated with us, and their own costs. I suggest you contact them directly with your request for a refund. I hope they provide you with a satisfactory response.

Yours sincerely

Liz Hard
Assistant Manager

How do I write a letter of complaint?

If you are writing a letter of complaint for your company it is very important to be polite and professional. Don't let annoyance tempt you into emotive language or sarcasm. Firmly and fairly request actions you would like the recipient to take.

Here is a good structure to follow for your letter:

1. Explain the specific incident precisely with details.
2. Describe the damage or defect.
3. Outline the implications of time or money lost, extra work created or inconvenience.
4. Ask for specific actions to remedy your complaint.

TROPICAL TANNING
11 Brown Street, Welburnt, Lancs, BL12 2FN
01234 432100

Mrs Flora Bloomfield   14 September 1998
Plant-you-Like
16 The High Street
Foilledge YO99 4XT

Dear Mrs Bloomfield

<u>Special Floral Display</u>

Several weeks ago I ordered a special floral display in the shape of a palm tree for the opening of our new beauty parlour.

Yesterday we took delivery of the order. The structure bore more resemblance to cactii than palm trees, and approximately 30% of the flowers and foliage used were clearly dying, and brown in colour.

This was not acceptable, so your delivery agent was asked to return the items to you. As a consequence our launch event lacked the visual impact and style we wished to create, and a great deal of money was wasted on invitations and canapes in the same theme.

I would like you to provide compensation so that we can relaunch the centre in a stylish manner.

Yours sincerely

Tania Legg
Manager

Are there any rules for letters to non-English speakers?

If you are writing to a company or person where English is not their first language, it's a very good idea to get advice. Specialist business translators exist, but most businesses operating internationally should be able to respond to letters written in clear English. Here is a checklist of things to look out for:

Names and salutations

There are different conventions for titles which you should find out about and use. For example:

English	French	Spanish	German
Mr	Monsieur (M)	Señor	Herr
Miss	Mademoiselle (Mlle)	Señorita	Fräulein
Mrs	Madame (Mme)	Señora	Frau

Special characters or letters

As you can see from the examples above, accents are used on certain letters, and it is polite to include them.

Clear language

As this book emphasises, always use the simplest language possible. When writing to people in other countries it is even more crucial to avoid analogies or complex sentences and jargon.

Cultural differences

It is important to find out about the acceptable means of address and tone or use of specific words. A businessman in New York would expect a very direct letter, in Saudi Arabia the same wording could cause offence. Here is an example: if you received a letter from the USA marketing a new fabric for hard-wearing pants – you'd probably think the writer was talking about underwear rather than trousers, and it would change the way you read the rest of the letter!

5. Where can I find out more?

What publications could I look at?

Reference books are always a wise investment. Make sure you have a good dictionary. Other references books are useful, particularly if you are writing a lot. Look for a thesaurus, grammar and etiquette guides. These are just some of the many publications available.

120 letters that get results, Consumers' Association 1991

Chambers English grammar, AJ Taylor, Chambers 1990

Clear English, Frank St George, Bloomsbury 1996

Dictionary of troublesome words, Bill Bryson, Penguin 1987

Instant business letters: 201 letters for every occasion, Ian Maitland, Thorsons 1996

Mastering communication, Nicky Stanton, Macmillan 1996

Mastering English grammar, SH Buon, Macmillan

Model business letters, Shirley Taylor, Pitman 1998

Modern English: A user's guide to grammar and style, Michael Beresford, Duckworth 1997

Plain English, Diane Collinson, Oxford University Press 1992

The complete idiot's almanac of business letters and memos, Tom Gorman, Alpha 1997

The Macmillan guide to English grammar, Rosalind Fergusson, Macmillan 1998

Usage and abusage: A guide to good English, Eric Partridge, Hamish Hamilton

Utter drivel, a decade of jargon and gobbledygook as recorded by the Plain English Campaign, Robson 1994

Is there any special training?

Some companies do run business communication courses for new recruits but they are few and far between. Many business training companies run one to two day courses, and some addresses are given below. However, the best experience you will get is by learning on the job – from your colleagues and managers.

A good starting point is to follow the guidelines set out in this book and look critically at the business letters you see as part of your job.

Who could I contact?

Spring's Pitman Training Group has offices throughout the UK. Check in your local telephone directory for contact details.

Business Training Ltd
Sevendale House, 7 Dale Street
Manchester M1 1JB
Tel: 0161 228 6735

Institute of Management
2 Savoy Court
London WC2
Tel: 0171 497 0580
http://www.inst-mgt.org.uk

Plain English Campaign
PO Box 3, New Mills
High Peak SK22 4QP
Tel: 01663 744409

The Word Centre
27 Norfolk Hill
Sheffield S3V 3QA
Tel: 0114 257 1400

After finishing university, you should be smart enough to spot a good deal when you see one.

As a graduate, we can offer you a first class package including:

- Special offers on graduate overdrafts and loans.
- Primeline, our 24 hour person-to-person telephone banking service.
- Commission-free travellers cheques and currency.
- And many other benefits.

If you'd like more details, simply call us on the number below.

0800 200 400
Monday-Friday 8am-8pm, Saturday 9am-6pm
www.natwest.co.uk

☘ NatWest
More than just a bank